Early Christianity
before the Romanization

by
JENNIE MOENCH

ᛉ

Warrior Publications, Inc.

Warrior Publications, Inc.
P.O. Box 127, Grand Blanc, Michigan 48480

Cover art by Jennie Lynn

ISBN 978-0-9854905-6-0

"Let him who seeks, not cease seeking until he finds, and when he finds, he will be troubled and when he has been troubled, he will marvel and he will reign over the all."

- Gospel of Thomas 80:14

Table of Contents

Introduction

The goal for me with this book, is to encourage people to look into ancient Christianity, and see what it looked like before changes were made by the Romans. I think that for the person who is truly open to new truths, this information will be interesting and exciting, and it will bring those progressive ancients, with their revolutionary ideas to life for the reader. And, that you might find out that we are not so different.

I try to clearly document references, so that you can judge for yourself. These Nag Hammadi documents are available to all online at no cost. I encourage you to read them for yourself.

Story of Nag Hammadi

In 1945 an Arab farmer digging for fertilizer near the Egyptian area of Nag Hammadi found a clay jar containing 13 leather bound papyrus codices with 52 Early Christian texts. So, what is written in these ancient text? That will be the topic of this book, written by an average person, after reading all available texts.

The literature was copied into Egyptian Coptic script, just before it was sealed into the jar and hidden in the earth. But why? To answer that, you first need to know the story of early Christianity, which begins in Alexandria, Egypt.

Alexandria was founded by Alexander the Great in 331 BC. It was located on the coast of the Mediterranean Sea and developed into an important trading hub with a large sea port. It became the intellectual capital of the Greek world, as all books that entered the port were copied and added to its magnificent library. By 290 BC it was the large source of knowledge. It attracted thinkers, dreamers, philosophers and literary giants of the ancient world. At a time before the printing press, easy travel, and communication, Alexandria was a hub of learning and progressive ideas.

It was at this time and place that the early Christian documents were written. These stories were written with a clearly antisemitic tone, or maybe the topic of Jewish mythology was a popular one at the time, I don't know. But, these Jesus stories and creation stories were imaginative and littered with Greek gods. And the religion that sprang from them was generous to other religions. Zoroaster and Buddha religions are embraced by many early Christians and mentioned in their literature, even respectfully blessed at the beginning of their sermons.

Then, as was the custom at the time, books were written in the voices of the individuals in their mythos. The Gospels of Thomas and Philip as well as Mark, Mathew, John, and Luke. Books were also written in the voice of even more ancient people like Adam, Eve, Norea and Seth. There came to be many differing Christian texts and many differing Christian sects, with differing points of view and ideas.

At first, Rome put it's nose up at the emerging Christian ideology. We have all read about the persecution of those early Christians by the Romans. But then, in 306 AD, Constantine becomes Romes new Emperor. He is the son of a Christian woman, Bithynia. At this time the Christian church had many members and some of them were well organized with branches in many ancient cities. In 313 AD, Constantine declares 'absolute toleration' of Christians and declares the cross a symbol of Christianity and requires it to be painted on the shields of his soldiers. Then in 325 AD the Council of Nicaea was given the power to settle disputes within the many differing Christian churches. It was decided which books were to be in the 'official' cannon of the Old and New Testaments, the

Bible. They also developed the Apostles Creed, which established official Roman Christian beliefs. New churches began to spring up, often displacing older churches. The site of an old temple to Aphrodite in Goligotha is declared the site of Jesus' tomb and the vast complex of the Holy Sepulchre is built.

Another interesting story concerning Alexander the Great happens during this time period. His body was interred in a tomb in his beloved Alexandria, it was visited by many famous people including Julius Caesar and Cleopatra, but then after mobs of Roman Christians invaded the city and destroyed all non-Roman Christian sites around 384 AD it disappears. But, what emerges is the found bones of St. Mark, one of the mythical Christian disciples. Interesting.

But, you see, this began happening everywhere. In 380 AD Roman Christianity is made the official state religion by Emperor Theodosius the Great, by 392 AD all other religions were banned, Roman Christianity was the ONLY religion allowed. Temples were destroyed, Roman Christian mobs leveled shrines and synagogues, and any books and writings that conflicted with the authorized version of Roman Christianity were burned.

When ignorance is embraced, terror reigns. Caesar may have accidentally burnt part of the Alexandrian library, but it was a casualty of a battle and not something that he would admit doing in historical documents, as everyone of his time had great respect for the libraries of Alexandria. But, sadly, not later, when the Roman Christian mobs, began destroying temples and burning books that contained information that they wanted to suppress, ideas that might conflict with the state.

And sadly, even two thousand years later, they are still at it! Whenever someone forbids you a book or listening to a lecture, that is exactly what you need to read and hear! You need to hear many points of view, freely discuss topics with others, and then you can make the best choices. If you are afraid that your child will become someone different than yourself, or acquire what you feel are bad ideas, try parenting not censorship. Ignorance should never be forced on anyone.

The internet is a modern Alexandria, you can find ancient books, the books referenced here, as well as the most current science, and it is available to all. This needs to be true, always.

But, back to the subject and the books of Nag Hammadi, because you see, there was a religious community there with many of these early, 'banned' books, and to keep them from the flame, they were copied into Egyptian Coptic writing before being hidden.

Those religious people who hid the books not only saved these books of knowledge from the fire, but the texts themselves may also hold clues about the story of what happened. There are forbidden books in the collection but also copies of letters and communications that representatives of the Church of Rome made after visiting the differing Christian sects. They were often written in a very derogatory way. With phrases like, "They say...", "They claim...", but what was difficult for me to read was when they would refer to the beloved Sophia as, 'the vile Sophia.' She is a very important character who will be discussed in the next section. After reading about her, her being slandered hurt my feelings! I can only imagine how the religious people who hid the books felt at the time. Roman Christianity was required, so, these Christians hid their beloved books with copies of their warrants.

The fact that fragments of Platos, Republic, was also with the other books, makes we wonder if the Roman Christian scourge that destroyed temples and writing about other gods might have been a mob, intent on censoring all progressive thinking that might have been on the fringes of what the religious mob considered correct.

But, one thing that needs to be mentioned here, is that almost all of the Nag Hammadi texts as well as most of the New Testament books, including the gospels, were all originally written in Greek, in fact, it was a dialect called, Koine, which was brought to Alexandria by Alexander the Great. So, the truth is, that Christianity was 'penned' in Egypt. In the great and progressive city of Alexandria, on the continent of Africa!

Story of Creation

As in the first book of John in the New Testament, the Christian story of creation starts before the creation of the Earth.

"In the beginning was the Word; the Word was in God's presence, and the Word was God. He was present to God in the beginning. Through him all things came into being, and apart from him nothing came to be. Whatever came to be in him, found life, life for the light of men. The light shines on in darkness, a darkness that did not overcome it." John (1:1-5)

Now, first, I want to prepare you for the cosmology in this story. It is everywhere! The ancients did understand the planets (spheres), their orbits, and even the existence of galaxies (aeons). The manuscripts sometimes read like science fiction!

In the Pistis Sophia book 1, chapter 52, Mary explains that: "the first then, who were created before us, are the invisibles, for indeed they arose before mankind, they and the gods and the rulers."

In book 2, chapter 86, Jesus introduces us to Sabaoth the Good, "Sabaoth, the good, whom I have called my father."

He is described in many places as androgynous, both male and female. At first, he was alone in the darkness, then he became acquainted with the Great Invisible Spirit, the Barbelo, that the Egyptian Gospel (54:19) describes as, "the masculine female virgin," who became pregnant and bore Jesus. And there you have it, the original holy trinity, father, mother and child. (We will discuss the progression of the trinity later in the book.)

Many other realms were created, and then, entities to rule over them. One of the most famous entities is Sophia. Her story, is documented well in the Pistis Sophia and other books, but it was the Pistis Sophia that was loved so much that it somehow escaped the Roman burning of books and was nearly the only existing book to tell the complete story of creation until the library of Nag Hammadi was discovered in 1945. In this book, Jesus tells her story to the Disciples.

I am telling this mainly from the Pistis Sophia, but it is repeated in many of the other texts. Sophia is not mentioned until chapter 29 of the first book, when Jesus explains, "I entered in into the thirteenth aeon and found Pistis Sophia below the thirteenth aeon all alone and no one of them with her."

She was grieving and mourning because she was not being admitted, as every entity had it's place in a hierarchy of aeons, and although you were allowed below your aeon, you were not allowed to go above it. But, she was ambitious and this caused the others to hate her. She is also curious and after Jesus leaves her, she sees the great light power of Yaldabaoth on a planet below her, she investigates.

Unfortunately, this is a trap that the jealous rulers have set up for her, and as she gets closer to the planet to observe the great lion-faced ruler, she is captured. They try to take her 'light-power,' and she fights them off and cries out. She can see the rulers of the aeons looking on, rejoicing at her peril. "I had done them no ill; but they hated me without a cause," she laments.

Even though Jesus seems to be concerned and wants to help her, his father refuses to allow him to rescue her until after she had lamented several times and sang several songs of praise. Only then, is Jesus allowed to send the angels, Gabriel and Michael. Jesus explains, "I gave unto them the light stream and let them go down into the chaos to help Pistis Sophia, and to take the light powers, which the emanations of Self-willed had taken from her, from them, and give them back to Pistis Sophia."

Finally, she is saved, but now, she is pregnant without her companion. This part is intriguing to me, as this woman is brave, and even though, she is ashamed of her condition, none the less, she wants to have the child. She hides her condition and then hides the child, who is born, "Serpentine with a lion's face," Secret Book of John (9:7.) He is given the name Ialtabaoth Saklas Samael and is raised alone, hidden in the clouds. He creates his own companions and

then, they help him create the Earth. He
becomes, "God of the Jews," IrBas (1.24.4).
"Creator of men," GJ (52:128.) The cruel and
wrathful, god of the old testament.

"This is the first ruler, and it took great power
from its mother, retreating from her and moved
out of the place where it had been born. Taking
possession of another place, it made for itself
other eternal realms inside a luminous, firery
blaze, which still exist. And it became stupefied
in its madness, which still is with it." - Secret
Book of John 9:19

But, Sabaoth the Good, Jesus' father, sees what
Ialtabaoth has done. He sees that he has made
man to be his slave, to be without his own will.
He placed them in a garden, but forbid them to
eat of the tree of knowledge. Then Sophia came
down to "rectify her lack."

"and thanks to it they tasted perfect
acquaintance....so that I might teach them and
raise them out of the depth of sleep." Secret
Book of John 23:25-31

In the Hypostasis of the Archons or Reality of
the Rulers it states about the creator "Their chief
is blind. Because of his power and his ignorance
and his arrogance he said, with his power, "I am

god; there is no other but me." When he said this, he sinned against all. This speech rose up to incorruptibility. Then there was a voice that came forth from incorruptibility, saying, "You are wrong, Samael," that is, god of the blind. His thoughts became blind."

In the more recently discovered, Gospel of Judas 54:137 "But God caused knowledge to be (given) to Adam and those with him, so that the kings of chaos and the underworld might not lord it over them."

So, it is Sabaoth as a snake that convinces Eve to eat from the tree of knowledge. It was Jesus' father, who gave us freewill. It was entities from his realm that encouraged a rebellion against their creator.

But, man continued to worship the cruel god, Ialtabaoth, who brought down a flood and caused many other hardships on the people. So, he sent his son, Jesus, to Earth. His mission was to convince the Jews to abandon their cruel god and follow his kind and loving father.

In the Second Apocalypse of James, he lectures those in Jerusalem that, "Your father is not my father." Then he urges them to, "know the father who has compassion."

In the beginning of Basilides' Myth, "Then the engendered, unnameable parent saw their ruin, and sent its first born, the intellect, called Christ, to save people who believed in it, from the authority of the beings that had crafted the world."

From there, the story of Jesus', birth, crucifixion, and life after his resurrection, are all told in a similar fashion in these, 'forbidden,' text, as well as, those gospels that were approved by the Romans for the New Testament.

Fate of the saviors of the library

They copied their beloved text into Egyptian Copic before burying them. I marvel at the humanity of those ancient Christians, who quickly copied and hid their beloved books to save them from the fires of Roman Christians. Could it be that they were afraid that if the books weren't in their libraries when the Romans came to burn them, then they would be accused of hiding them? While reading and re-reading these ancient texts, I begin to get a sense of what they must have been going through.

Their lives were being disrupted because they refused to conform to Roman Christianity. Their books burned, their churches and temples destroyed. They were being forced to take the Roman's creed and denounce the religious ideas that they had been brought up believing, whether they were Christian or any other religion as the Roman mobs were destroying everything that didn't conform to the new Roman religion.

I grew to love the stories of creation and especially Sophia, the brave female whose curiosity caused her to be captured by the cruel Adamas. Then, those other more recent letters that appear to be written by someone from the Roman church reporting on the unauthorized beliefs and books being used. They recounted the same stories, but with malice and would refer to Sophia as 'the vile Sophia.' This hurt my feelings! I can't imagine how it would have been for those religious people. But, then, I did come across another writing, which I believe may have been a written response to the accusations of false doctrine and the insults to Sophia.

The Second Treatise of the Great Seth, third paragraph: "For those who were in the world had been prepared by the will of our sister Sophia – she who is a whore – because of the innocence which has not been uttered. And she did not ask anything from the All, nor from the greatness of the Assembly, nor from the Pleroma. Since she was first, she came forth to prepare monads and places for the Son of Light…"

Then, in the last paragraph: "I am Jesus Christ, the son of Man… But I alone am the friend of Sophia. I have been in the bosom of the father from the beginning, in the place of the sons of truth, and the Greatness."

At first, I asked myself, why did they bother including those letters that condemned them? I wondered about it, and then realized, that by including these texts, those people were telling their own story of what happened to them and the reason why they were hiding these books in jars and burying them. They lived in tumultuous times, it must have been terrifying! So, maybe this war against knowledge and diversity of thought that we find ourselves in now, is a fight that has been in progress for 2,000 years. How many can say that they feel safe refuting anything about Roman Christianity, to this day!

Alexandria

Two thousand years ago, Alexandria would have been the place that everyone dreamed of living. Philosophy and all things creative where discussed in open. Their library was the marvel of the world and included copies of books from every ship that entered its seaport. Ideas were available and discussed freely, those religions of the Egyptians as well as the Greeks, Jews, Zoroaster, Hindu, and Buddhist were all influential, and from this, came the birth of Christianity. The mysticism and the Jesus stories.

I have to say, to me, the early creation story and some of the themes in the Gospels are based in antisemitic ideas, it feels to me as though they may have been written by an angry adult who was raised Jewish. But, the Gospels were stories about a demigod who was born on Earth, how he lived and interacted with people, he was caring, and loving, and represented the best in humanity. He was someone that we all need to imitate. I can see why the Jesus stories became so popular.

And then, began the writings that were inspired by the characters in the stories, like fan fiction, each telling tales from their point of view. And, there were many! More than the few that the

Roman's included in their collection. As, I'm sure, there are even more being produced to this day. Alexandria would have been a haven for anyone who wrote or appreciated literature, philosophy and knowledge.

And, then, came the book burners.

Apostles Creed

In 325 AD, the Council of Nicaea, was held in what is now Iznik, Turkey, there, it was determined which books would be in the new Christian bible. They also created the Apostles Creed, which outlined the important beliefs that Roman Christianity would espouse. By, the mid forth century, it was more than a suggestion, it was a requirement.

Below is a copy of the original creed in 325 AD:

I believe in God, the Father Almighty,
Creator of Heaven and earth;
and in Jesus Christ, His only Son, Our Lord,
Who was conceived by the Holy Ghost,
born of the Virgin Mary,
suffered under Pontius Pilate,
was crucified; died, and was buried.

Newer version from 8th century:

I believe in one God, the Father almighty,
Creator of heaven and earth.
I believe in Jesus Christ, his only son, our Lord,
who was conceived by the Holy Spirit
and born of the virgin Mary.
He suffered under Pontius Pilate,
was crucified, died, and was buried;
he descended to hell.
The third day he rose again from the dead.
He ascended to heaven.
and is seated at the right hand of God the Father
almighty.
From there he will come to judge the living and
the dead.
I believe in the Holy Spirit,
the holy catholic church,
the communion of saints,
the forgiveness of sins,
the resurrection of the body,
and the life everlasting. Amen.

I believe in (one) God, the Father almighty,

If you read the creation story above, you can see
that this first line is a problem, as the early
Christians always believed in at least two gods,
Jesus' father and the creator, with the two being
very distinct from one another. This

fundamental change must have been very difficult. Why did Christianity need to be monotheistic anyway? I wondered if maybe there was a powerful Jewish influence at the time, as the Romans seemed to be pulling Christianity closer to its Jewish roots. Could this be to appease Jewish interests?

Another reason that came to my mind, was that I thought about what religions Christianity would be replacing, mostly, the Greek and Roman pantheon of gods. Could the reason for monotheism be, to keep those old gods out of the picture? If this clause wasn't in the contract, would less enthusiastic new Christians simply add Jesus and his father to their existing list of gods? I think this is very possible. In the Nag Hammadi texts, you will find references to Zeus, Aphrodite, Hades, the list goes on and on. So, obviously the old gods were not a problem for the early Christians, until the Romans made it an issue.

Creator of heaven and earth.

Well, that lets you know which god won out! Clearly, the Romans wanted you to worship the creator god. The god of the old testament, maybe that is why the Christian bible also includes the old Jewish books of the 'old testament,' as well as the new. Somehow you are supposed to believe the old and new testament god is the same.

I believe in Jesus Christ, his only son, our Lord,

For me, this is interesting, as they are reinforcing the idea of a demigod in Jesus, yet they don't want to call him that. That would sound too….Greek? Yet, with this line, they are admitting to two gods. Jesus and his father. But, you are not allowed to say that. So…whatever.

who was conceived by the Holy Ghost and born of the virgin Mary.

Now this bit was, also, very controversial, as in the beginning, the trinity was Father, Mother, Son. Remember the Great Invisible Spirit that gave birth to Jesus in the beginning? The Mother?

The Egyptian Gospel 50:23 "Three powers emanated from it: namely the father, the mother, and the son"

Trimorphic Protennoia (about ¾ through) "Thought exists as three permanences: the Father, the Mother, the Son"

Then, in other texts, Jesus is described as the 'triple -male' as in Allogenes toward the beginning. And as the 'thrice male' in the Three Tablets of Seth. There were many other references like this, which I believe would be a correct description after the holy spirit became male.

Early Christianity was full of important women, until it was Romanized. Many disciples were women, Salome, Mary, Martha, Arsinoe, Mariam, are all mentioned. In Pistis Sophia they are seated with the other disciples while Jesus encourages discussion. In fact, Mary is so enthusiastic in discussions that Peter becomes annoyed and complains that she is dominating the conversation.

Peter speaking, Pistis Sophia book 1, 36:57 "My Lord, we will not endure this woman, for she taketh the opportunity from us and hath let none of us speak, but she discourseth many times."

Which causes Mary to hesitate in the 2 book of the Pistis Sophia 72:161 "I am afraid of Peter, because he threatened me and hateth our sex."

Salome is mentioned as one of the disciples seated before Jesus in discussions in the first book of the Pistis Sophia 54:102, 58:114, in book four 132:342, in book six 145:381.

In the Gospel According to Thomas 91:24 "Salome said: Who art thou, man, and (…) whose (son)? Thou didst take thy place upon my bench and eat from my table. Jesus said to her: I am He"

Martha is mentioned by name in the first book of the Pistis Sophia 38:61 and 57:111. Then again in the second book, 73:162 and 80:174

And the reduction of females in Roman Christianity continued until there were almost none! Peter was the rock that the Roman church was built on, and his misogyny appears to have won out. But the women disciples are also mentioned by name on the last page of the First Apocalypse of James.

Then, there were the angels and rulers of heavenly realms like, Ennoias, Paraplex, Hekate, Persephone, this list is very long. When you read about the first entities, you find out that they were androgynous, often having a male and a female name.

What happened? Well, this was one of my big questions going into this project. What happened to the women? What I noticed, is that they seem to have changed sex about the same time that the Holy Spirit became male. There was controversy about it then, too.

The Gospel of Phillip 14:23 "Some said that Mary conceived by the holy spirit: they are mistaken, they do not realize what they say. When did a female ever conceive by a female?"

So, I still don't understand why the holy spirit became male and why women were all but erased from Christianity, but I see that it happened.

He suffered under Pontius Pilate,

This is interesting, as it isn't mentioned anywhere, but in the New Testament books. It almost makes me wonder if Pontius Pilate was added to verify the time period that Jesus was supposed to live in. Time was not tied to the birth of Jesus until the Romans decided that the Jesus stories were historical. It was then, in the middle of the forth century, that it was decided that Jesus' birth marked year zero.

was crucified, died, and was buried;

This doesn't seem to be disputed, other than some sects, who claimed that he wasn't crucified, but rather the person who carried his cross, Simon, was the crucified one. But, the time period that he was on Earth after his crucifixion was the setting for much of his discourse.

In the eighth century the rest was added under Charlemagne:

From there he will come to judge the living and the dead.

In the sixth book of the Pistis Sophia, Jesus explains what happens when a good person dies. First, you are led with joy to Bainchoooch, who spends three days circling the Earth with them. Then, they are led to the Virgin of Light to be judged. The soul is then given a cup of forgetfulness and tossed back to the Earth to be reincarnated.

I believe in the Holy Spirit,
the holy catholic church,
the communion of saints,
the forgiveness of sins,
the resurrection of the body,
and the life everlasting. Amen.

Lastly, the person reciting the Creed affirms their fealty to the Holy Spirit and the holy Catholic Church. Note that the word catholic means universal.

Different Christian Sects

There did evolve different Christian Sects. During this time of no mass communication, many people received their first lessons on Christianity from whichever Christian was handy. Some worshiped Seth, Adam's son, in place of Jesus. These people called themselves 'Sethian.' I wonder if the Egyptian god, Set, (or Seth,) was in the mix.

Another Christian Sect that Jesus condemns in the sixth book of Pistis Sophia 147:386, practiced a strange ritual that included making a lentil porridge out of semen and a woman's monthly blood. When Thomas describes this, Jesus becomes angry and says that their souls will be destroyed. So, there was infighting between Christians without Roman interference, as well.

St. Epiphanius describes in The Gnostics 26.3.7 a sex cult that believed that orgasm brought them closer to god. Everyone, even women, were free to have sex with anyone as long as the man didn't ejaculate into the woman, she was still considered a virgin. Sex parties were held, even for strangers if they knew the signal, which was for the visitor to tickle the palm of parishioner upon shaking hands, this admitted them into the orgy.

Now, according to this St. Epiphanius, who was clearly a spy, collecting unauthorized beliefs and books, these same sex craved Christians also cannibalized aborted fetuses. Who knows!

But, for me, it was easy to see Greek and Egyptian influences all through the documents. Zoroaster and Buddhist ideals were also present. In studying Mani, (216-276 AD) and the large Manichaean Christian church that he founded, I read in hymn after hymn where leaders of their church were praised along side Buddhist, Hindu and Zoroaster leaders. Everyone was blessed. The religions appeared to live in harmony.

The Three Marys

Throughout my reading, sorting out the Marys was always a chore, as sometimes his mother is indicated and sometimes Mary of Magdalene is specified, but it isn't always clear, until I read this:

Philip 28:6 "Three women used to walk with the lord. Mary his mother, his sister and the Magdalene, who is called his companion."

Note that in the new testament, in the book of John, there are five instances where 'the disciple who Jesus loved,' is mentioned. I personally believe this is Mary Magdalene, as she is often described as his companion, but, for whatever reason, the Romans decided that Jesus was to be celibate, so it is suspicious to me. I think her second rate status is due to her sex.

In all other early Christian books, Mary of Magdalene is Jesus' companion and nowhere is she called a prostitute. In fact, that sounds like something that Sophia would have been called by the Romans. They slander the women and then erase them. But, here is a more common references to her:

Philip 48:32 "And the companion of the (…) Mary Magdalene. The (…loved) her more than the disciples, (and he used to) kiss her often than the rest of the disciples. They said to him, "why do you love her more than all of us?" The savior answered, saying to them, "Why do I not love you like her? If a blind person and one with sight are both in darkness they are not different from one another. When the light comes, then the person with sight will see the light, and the blind person will remain in the darkness."

Jesus and a story not in bible

He is described in almost every book, in the same fashion that he is described in the New Testament. I did come across a story about young Jesus, in the first book of the Pistis Sophia chapter 61, Mary, Jesus' mother, tells a story:

"When thou wert little, before the spirit had come upon thee, whilst thou wert in a vineyard with Joseph, the spirit came out of the height and came to me in my house, like unto thee; and I did not know him, but I thought that thou wast he. And the spirit said unto me: 'Where is Jesus, my brother, that I meet with him?' And when he had said this unto me, I was at a loss and thought it was a phantom to try me. So I seized him and bound him to the foot of the bed in my house, until I went forth to you, to thee and Joseph in the field, and I found you on the vineyard, Joseph propping up the vineyard. It came to pass, therefore, when thou didst hear me speak the word unto Joseph, that thou didst understand the word, wert joyful and saidest: 'Where is he, that I may see him; else I await him in this place.' And it came to pass, when

Joseph had heard thee say these words, that he
was startled. And we went down together,
entered the house and found the spirit bound to
the bed. And we looked on thee and him and
found thee like unto him. And he who was
bound to the bed was unloosed: he took thee in
his arms and kissed thee, and thou also didst
kiss him. Ye became one."

James

Is sometimes referred to as Jesus' brother, but
toward the beginning of the First Apocalypse of
James, Jesus says, "for not without reason have
I called you my brother, although you are not
my brother maternally."

Then toward the beginning of the Second
Apocalypse of James, James' mother explains,
"Do not be frightened, my son, because he said
'my brother' to you. For you were nourished
with this same milk. Because of this he calls me
'my mother". For he is not a stranger to us. He
is your step-brother."

Levi

In the more recent discovery, The Gospel of
Mary, she describes him as her defender in the
eighteenth chapter. "Levi answered and said to

Peter, "Peter, you always are angry. Now I see you arguing against this woman like an adversary. If the savior made her worthy, who are you to reject her? Surely the savior knows her well. That is why he has loved her more than us.""

In the First Apocalypse of James he is mentioned again, but, so many of the words in these passages are missing, it makes it difficult to determine if this is about the same person.

Thomas

In the Sixth book of Pistis Sophia, concerning the spell that other Christian sects were preforming, Thomas is the one who reports this to Jesus.

At the beginning of the Book of Thomas the Contender, Jesus says, "Now, since it has been said that you are my twin and true companion, examine yourself, and learn who you are, in what way you exist, and how you will come to be. Since you will be called my brother, it is not fitting that you be ignorant of yourself."

Solomon

There is an interesting story about Solomon, toward the end of The Testimony of Truth.

"Others have demons dwelling with them, as did David the king. He is the one who laid the foundation of Jerusalem; and his son Solomon, who he begot in adultery, is the one who built Jerusalem by means of the demons, because he received power. When he had finished building, he imprisoned the demons in the temple. He placed them into seven waterpots. They remained a long time in the waterpots, abandoned there. When the Romans went up to Jerusalem, they discovered the waterpots, and immediately the demons ran out of the waterpots, as those who escaped from prison."

This intrigued me, as I had never heard this story, so I did some research and found another reference to this story in the 'Book of the Archangels by Moses the Prophet' (not Nag Hammadi,) which turns out to be a book about magic, that also references 'The Testament of Solomon,' another book of magic. So, when I found this:

The Revelation of Adam 79:3, "Solomon, too, sent his army of demons to search for the female virgin."

and this in The Apocalypse of Adam near the middle: "Solomon himself sent his army of demons to seek out the virgin."

In these stories Solomon is the bad guy with demons trying to prevent the birth of Jesus. Wasn't some of that blamed on Herod in the book of Matthew?

Norea

Eve's daughter, who is still alive when Noah is building his ark, has an interesting story that I remember reading at least twice.

In the Hypostasis of the Archons, in about the middle, this story is told:

"Then Norea came to him, wanting to board the ark. And when he would not let her, she blew upon the ark and caused it to be consumed by fire. Again he made the ark, for a second time."

Zeus

In the fifth book of the Pistis Sophia in chapter
140:

"And when the sphere turneth itself and the little
Sabaoth, the good, who is called in the world
Zeus"

In Asclepius toward the end: "Now the creator
has control in the place that is between the earth
and heaven. He is called 'Zeus', that is, 'life'.
Plutonius Zeus is lord over the earth and sea.

The people who live under the Earth

When studying these 2,000 year old texts, I am
often surprised how they read like a science
fiction story. In the first book of Pistis Sophia in
chapter 12, when Jesus describes space and the
planets that he encounters, I was surprised when
he mentioned that some of the planets had life
inside of them. It seemed to indicate that people
living underground was normal. But, then I
encountered another casual reference in
Marsanes, near the end.

"and these numbers (people), whether those in heaven or those upon the earth, together with those that are under the earth,..."

I was intrigued.

Then I came across another mention in the first part of Melchizedek.

"But those in the heavens spoke many words, together with those on the earth, and those under the earth..."

Now, this all might have gotten passed me if it wasn't for all that I'd read about Cappodocia in Turkey. There are large underground complexes, cities connected by tunnels. There are also the remains of underground cities in Italy, Jordan and France. They were all in use during these early days of Christianity and often included Christian churches. Could the references to those under the earth be speaking of these people? Remember, we are discussing documents that were mainly written in the area of Alexandria, where books from all over the world were readily available.

Enlightenment

Although only fragments of the Pistis Sophia were found at Nag Hammadi, fortunately the entire book somehow escaped the flames! I have read it several times. It is a difficult read, especially, the first time. It is filled with wonderful descriptions of space, told by Jesus to his disciples.

Pistis Sophia, book 2 84:185 Jesus when asked to describe space: "ye will deem this world before you as darkness of darkness, and ye will look at the whole world of men, how it will have the condition of a speck of dust for you because of the great distance it is, far distant from it, and because of the great condition it is considerably greater than it."

Remember, this was written 2,000 years ago. Even for those who translated this particular book in the 1800s, no one had been to space so the words necessary to describe it, didn't exist.

Pistis Sophia, book 2, 88:199 Jesus explains, "there existeth no manner to describe it in this world."

Yet, he does, using words and descriptions available. Now, at this point, I'm sure some will be shouting, "Aliens!" Well, those are also described, but if you continue to read, you will find him again and again telling those disciples around him that this view is available to everyone after they learn the great mysteries. Enlightenment. While he is being questioned by his disciples it becomes clear that anyone, even unholy people, can achieve this type of enlightenment that causes their soul to astral project into space! Where, there are many different entities. Some living on great spheres, some living inside them.

In the first part of the Apocalypse of Paul, the Holy Spirit takes him up and says, "Look and see your likeness upon the earth? And he looked down and saw those who were upon the earth."

The collection has a few books written by 'enlightened' individuals.

Stories about space

Pistis Sophia book 1, 2:5 "And that light power came down over Jesus and surrounded him entirely..."
The story continues with Jesus being lifted up into the heavens and returned the next day. But when he returned he was so bright that no one could look at him. So, he "drew to himself the glory of his light," so that they could look at him. Jesus then comforted them by telling them that he had, "gone to the regions out of which I had come forth."

In Pistis Sophia book 1, 15:25 When Jesus lands on the planet of the evil Adamas, who began a fight with Jesus even though he didn't know who he was fighting with, as he could only see the light. So, Jesus took 1/3 of his power and then changed the motion of his planet so that he could not accomplish his evil influences on other planets.

Then, Mary commenting on his words, "'I have taken a third from the power of the rulers of all the aeons, and changed their fate and their sphere over which they rule, in order that, if the race of men invoke them in the mysteries – those which the angels who transgressed have taught them for the accomplishing of their evil and lawless deeds in the mystery of their sorcery,' in order then that they may no more from this hour accomplish their lawless deeds, because thou hast taken their power from them and from their horoscope casters and their consulters and from those who declare to the men in the world all things which shall come to pass in order that they should no more, from this hour, know how to declare unto them anything at all which will come to pass." Then a few lines down she says, "Where then, O Egypt, where are thy consulters and horoscope casters..." making me believe that Egypt was the subject of this whole bit.

Zostrianos 4:20 "Now, after it (the angel) said these words, in its company with eagerness and great gladness I went on board a large luminous cloud, leaving my modeled form on earth guarded by glories. And escaped from the whole world and the thirteen realms residing in it, host of angels, without our being seen. And their ruler was troubled by (our) journey. For, the cloud being far superior (to any) worldly thing; It had ineffable beauty; glowed; was powerful; led the way for holy spirits; and existed as a life giving spirit an intellectual utterance."

At the end of Melchizedek: "When the brethren who belong to the generations of life had said these things, they were taken up to above all the heavens."

Another interesting story about Melchisedec happens in book 1 of the Pistis Sophia, chapter 25, when dealing with evil rulers "he set in motion the hastener who is over them, and made them turn their circles swiftly, and he carried away their power which was in them and the breath of their mouth and the tears of their eyes and the sweat of their bodies." Then Melchiesedec took the "souls of men and cattle and reptiles and wild beasts and birds, and send them down into the world of mankind."

Another thing that I found interesting is the common uses of the Zodiac. Now, according to google it is not used in its current form until the middle ages yet…

In the fifth book of the Pistis Sophia, chapter 139 discusses the houses and constellations giving them the numbers and names that we use now. These came from Greek mythology, so I guess I'm slightly less surprised. But, one thing, for sure, is that those who claim that people 2,000 years ago thought the world was flat, well, they are as confused as the people in the 21st century who claim the same thing.

Chants

I came across several references to chants used for meditation.

Allogenes about mid way: "The power appeared by means of an activity that is at rest and silent, although it uttered a sound thus: zza zza zza."

Marsanes about 2/3 in: "The third shape of the soul is (unknown) is a spherical one, put after it, from the simple vowels: eee, iii, ooo, uuu, OOO. The diphthongs were as follows: ai, au, ei, ui Oi auei, euEu, oiou, ggg, ggg, ggg, aiau, eieu, Eu, oiou, Ou, ggg, ggg, aueieu, oiou, Eu, three times for a male soul...." This continues and appears to be a kind of spell to summon the gods.

The Discourse on the Eight and Ninth is full of chants and vocalizations as is the Egyptian Gospel.

Reincarnation

In the first book of Pistis Sophia, Jesus explains to his disciples that he took twelve souls from the treasury of the Light so that these souls would be born on earth.

Pistis Sophia 7:11 "I brought from the beginning with me twelve powers...These then I cast into the womb of your mothers, when I came into the world, that is those which are in your bodies today."

Then, as in the new testament, Jesus explains how John the Baptist was the reincarnation of Elias.

Pistis Sophia 7:12 "I found Elizabeth, the mother of John the Baptizer, before she had conceived him, and I sowed into her a power which I had received from the little Iao, the

Good, who is in the Midst, that he might be able to make proclamation before me and make ready my way, and baptize with the water of forgiveness of sins. That power than is in the body of John.

"Moreover in place of the soul of the rulers which he was appointed to receive, I found the soul of the prophet Elias in the aeons of the sphere; and I took him thence, and took his soul and brought it to the Virgin of Light, and she gave it over to her receivers; they brought it to the sphere of the rulers and cast it into the womb of Elizabeth."

Then in the second book of Pistis Sophia 100:251 "Your being poured from one into another of different kinds of bodies..."

The Apocalypse of Paul, about half through, "The soul that had been cast down went to a body which had been prepared for it."

Hell

I have often heard people say that hell was invented more recently. This isn't quite true, as 'Hades' (Greek) is referred to often, as is 'Tartarus,' (Roman.)

Circumcision

In the Gospel According to Thomas, Jesus is asked if circumcision was profitable.

Thomas 90:20 "If it were profitable, their father would beget them circumcised from their mother."

Charging interesting

Jesus says in Thomas 97 "If you have money, do not lend at interest, but give to him from whom you will not receive them (back.)"

Abortion

I think many people are under the impression that abortion is a modern thing. Nope.

In, The Origin of the World, toward the beginning, speaking of the birth of Ialtabaoth. "like an aborted fetus since there was no spirit in it."

So, it appears that the soul doesn't enter the body until after birth.

Philip 67:8 "When we were born we were
joined."

There are many instances where abortion is
mentioned, but never do any of the text claim
that you are a whole person before you are born.
I believe Jewish texts are similar. So, to claim
that abortion is the murder of a person, would be
considered ridiculous to an early Christian.

Dragons

About 2/3 through the Apocalypse of Adam: "It
came from heaven to earth Dragons brought him
down to caves."

Revelation of Adam 80:13 "Dragons took him
down into their dens, and he became a servent."

Then, I came across another old book, but not
found in Nag Hammadi, it was called the Hymn
of the Pearl, in which there is an entire story
about a dragon.

We need critical thinking

Everyone needs to be free to pursue knowledge
and truth, and to debate ideas without fear. This

is necessary for developing critical thinking. We need to be able to identify all of our options so that we can make decisions. Otherwise, we cease to think, and then, like dumb animals, we simply obey the loudest voice.

Final Thoughts

Being a typical American, living in this twenty-first century, I think the most surprising thing for me to learn was that Jesus was a mythical being. I had always just assumed that the stories in the new testament were historical documents, because that was what we have been taught for 2,000 years! But, if you study the old religions of the Hindu, Egyptians, Greeks and Romans, those people didn't believe all of their mythology literally! Buddhism is full of wonderful stories about the Buddha and his incarnations and just as with the stories of Jesus, they are stories of inspirational people giving good advice. As their authors intended. One of the first 'literal' religions has to be Jewish, and, I'm not convinced that it wasn't also the Romans who determined that for them. But one thing that I feel confident of, and am proud of, is knowing that Jesus was born in the Greek literature of Alexandria.

www.ingramcontent.com/pod-product-compliance
Lightning Source LLC
Chambersburg PA
CBHW060624030426
42337CB00018B/3177